Pebble® Plus

SEA LIFE

SEA LIONS

by **Elizabeth R. Johnson**

Consultant:
Jody Rake, Member,

Southwest Marine Educators Association

CAPSTONE PRESS
a capstone imprint

Pebble Plus is published by Capstone Press,
1710 Roe Crest Drive, North Mankato, Minnesota 56003
www.mycapstone.com

Library of Congress Cataloging-in-Publication Data
Names: Johnson, Elizabeth R., 1986–author.
Title: Sea lions / by Elizabeth R. Johnson.
Other titles: Pebble plus. Sea life.
Description: North Mankato, Minnesota : Capstone Press, [2017] | Series:
  Pebble plus. Sea life | Audience: Ages 4–8. | Audience: K to grade 3. |
  Includes bibliographical references and index.
Identifiers: LCCN 2016005488| ISBN 9781515720829 (library binding) | ISBN
  9781515720867 (eBook PDF)
Subjects: LCSH: Sea lions—Juvenile literature.
Classification: LCC QL737.P63 J62 2017 | DDC 599.79/75—dc23
LC record available at http://lccn.loc.gov/2016005488

Editorial Credits
Jaclyn Jaycox, editor; Philippa Jenkins, designer;
Svetlana Zhurkin, media researcher; Gene Bentdahl, production specialist

Photo Credits
iStockphoto: mrbfaust, cover; Minden Pictures: Michael Quinton, 17, Michio Hoshino, 7; Shutterstock: A.F.Smith, 5, Andrey Gudkov, 9, 15, Bildagentur Zoonar GmbH, 19, chbaum, 13, Christian Musat, 11, Eric Isselee, back cover, 3, 6, 24, Longjourneys, 21

Design Elements by Shutterstock

Note to Parents and Teachers

The Sea Life set supports national science standards related to life science. This book describes and illustrates sea lions. The images support early readers in understanding the text. The repetition of words and phrases helps early readers learn new words. This book also introduces early readers to subject-specific vocabulary words, which are defined in the Glossary section. Early readers may need assistance to read some words and to use the Table of Contents, Glossary, Read More, Internet Sites, and Index sections of the book.

Printed in China.
022016   007718

Table of Contents

Life in the Ocean

Look at that sea lion gliding through the waves! There are six kinds of sea lions. They all live along the Pacific Ocean coast.

Sea Lion Range

where sea lions live

Sea lions spend time in large groups. A group of sea lions in the ocean is called a raft.

Sea lions are loud!
They bark, honk, and roar.
A pup can pick out its mother's
bark in a large group.

Up Close

Sea lions are related to seals and look like them. But they have differences too. Sea lions have earflaps. Seals just have very small ear openings.

earflap

Sea lions are big animals.

The largest sea lions weigh up to

2,469 pounds (1,120 kilograms)!

Sea lions are strong swimmers. They use flippers to swim and walk. A sea lion's coat is waterproof. Underneath is a thick layer of blubber for warmth.

flippers

Finding Food

Sea lions eat fish and squid.
They also like crabs and clams.
Sea lions dive deep under water
to find food. They can hold their
breath for 10 to 20 minutes!

Life Cycle

Sea lions leave the ocean to mate and give birth. Newborn pups drink their mother's milk. They have a fuzzy coat of hair to keep warm.

After a few weeks, pups learn to swim and hunt. They stay with their mother for up to one year. In the wild, sea lions live up to 30 years.

Glossary

blubber—a thick layer of fat under the skin of some animals; blubber keeps animals warm

coast—land next to an ocean or sea

flipper—one of the broad, flat limbs of a sea lion that help it swim

glide—to move smoothly and easily

mate—to join with another to produce young; a mate is also the male or female partner of a pair of animals

waterproof—able to keep water out

Read More

Peterson, Megan Cooley. *California Sea Lions*. Marine Mammals. Mankato, Minn.: Capstone Press, 2013.

Riggs, Kate. *Sea Lions. Amazing Animals*. Mankato, Minn.: Creative Education, 2014.

Silverman, Buffy. *Can You Tell a Seal from a Sea Lion?* Animal Look-alikes. Minneapolis: Lerner, 2012.

Internet Sites

FactHound offers a safe, fun way to find Internet sites related to this book. All of the sites on FactHound have been researched by our staff.

Here's all you do:

Visit *www.facthound.com*

Type in this code: 9781515720829

Check out projects, games and lots more at
www.capstonekids.com

Index